LIBRARIES AND INFORMATION CENTERS WITHIN WOMEN'S STUDIES RESEARCH CENTERS

by Grace Jackson-Brown

SLA RESEARCH SERIES
No. 3

1988

Special Libraries Association Washington, D.C.

Contents

Acknowledgments

1. Defining Women's Studies Research Centers..1
2. An Overview of Women's Studies Research Centers 3
3. Libraries and Information Centers Within Women's
   Studies Research Centers..10
4. Advocacy and Women's Studies Research Centers 19
5. Publishing and Women's Studies Research Centers 22
6. A National Women's Research Database...25

Appendix

Copyright © 1988 by Special Libraries Association
1700 Eighteenth Street, N.W., Washington, D.C. 20009

Manufactured in the United States of America
All rights reserved
ISBN 0–87111–333–3

Acknowledgments

The author wishes to express her gratitude to the many centers that answered her queries, and for the contributions of their catalogs, annual reports, and other information. The process of gathering, compiling and analyzing this data and information took nearly a year. The writing and revising of the actual book manuscript took almost another year. The author extends her warmest and most sincere gratitude to the many friends and professional associates who supported her in this effort.

CHAPTER ONE
Defining Women's Studies Research Centers

Women's Studies Research Centers (WSRCs) originated from the contemporary feminist and women's studies movements in the United States.[1] As organizations they form a powerful information network that provides institutional resources for research by, for, and about women.[2] According to Mariam Chamberlain, president of the National Council for Research on Women,

> Collectively they (WSRCs) provide institutional resources for research on women that supplement the efforts of individual scholars and make possible the development of large-scale and interdisciplinary research programs. The results of the research activities of the centers have not only been used as materials for women's studies courses but have also been brought to bear on the formation of public policy.[3]

This book will focus chiefly on the role of libraries and information centers that conduct women's studies research. The role of these special libraries and information centers is proactive in the development of feminist research, in influencing public policy, and in building and promoting women's studies as an academic discipline.

Shelia Tobias, a leading scholar in the field of women's studies and the development of WSRCs, defines women's studies this way:

> Women's studies is the intellectual examination of the absence of women from history; a fresh look in a non-Freudian way at the social psychology of women; the study of women in literature and the images of women in the Arts; the economic and legal history of the family; and speculation about "androgeny," a state of society and a state of mind where sex differences might be socially, economically, and politically overcome.[4]

Women's studies have received academic recognition only since the mid-1970s. It is a growing and evolving field that continues to prosper despite a politically controversial and academically tentative history. In 1984, there were some 480 degree-granting women's studies programs offered by colleges and universities across the United States, along with thousands of other colleges and universities that offer women's studies courses.[5]

The National Council for Research on Women reported in 1985 that 45 women's research centers and organizations were members of the Council.[6] This is the primary group of WSRCs that will be discussed in the following chapters. (*See* the WSRCs Directory, Appendix.) Given the definitions of WSRCs and women's studies by Chamberlain and Tobias, respectively, all of the organizations to be discussed fit most, if not all, of the established criteria of a WSRC.

References

1. Mariam Chamberlain, "A Period of Remarkable Growth: Women's Studies Research Centers," *Change*, 14 (1984), pp. 24–29.

   Mary Evans, "Women's Studies Research in the United States: A Review and Discussion," *Women's Studies International Quarterly*, 4 (1981), pp. 221–224.

   Hanna-Beate Schopp-Schilling, "Women's Studies, Women's Research and Women's Research Centres: Recent Developments in the U.S.A. and F.R.G.," *Women's Studies International Quarterly*, 2 (1978), pp. 103–116.

2. *Ibid.*

3. Chamberlain, "A Period of Remarkable Growth," p. 24.

4. Shelia Tobias, "Women's Studies: Its Origins, Its Organization and Its Prospects," *Women's Studies International Quarterly*, 1 (1978), p. 85.

5. National Women's Studies Association, *Newsletter*, 2 (Fall 1984), p. 27.

6. (Mariam Chamberlain), "National Council for Research on Women," *Women's Studies Quarterly*, 1 (Spring 1985), pp. 33–45.

CHAPTER TWO

An Overview of Women's Studies Research Centers

Lists of WSRCs were published in three national journals in 1979, 1982, and 1985.[1] The latest of these WSRC directories, compiled by the National Council for Research on Women, appeared in *Women's Studies Quarterly*, Spring 1985. In each reported year, the number of WSRCs grew, and references were made to important library collections and information centers at a number of them. Between 1974 and 1981, several articles were published in professional library literature about the Schlesinger Library and the Henry A. Murray Research Center at Radcliffe.[2] In 1986, Susan B. Hildenbran edited a book entitled *Women's Collections: Libraries, Archives, and Consciousness*, which spotlighted some of the key women's collections.

The purpose of the study herein described was to explore the present role of libraries and information centers within major WSRCs in the United States. A questionnaire, "Libraries and Information Centers Within Women's Studies Research Centers Survey," was mailed to directors or designated contact persons at major WSRCs on February 21, 1986. A follow-up letter was sent on March 11, 1986. The name list for the survey was developed by using the directory of the National Council for Research on Women and a publication of the Women's Research and Education Institute (WREI) titled *A Directory of Selected Women's Research and Policy Centers*.[3]

The two directories provided a means to verify the name and address information of important centers. Only three names that were listed in the WREI directory were not found in the national Council for Research on Women compilation. These three names were added to the survey sample, making a total of 45 WSRCs in the survey.

Thirty-five of the WSRCs, or 77.7 percent, responded to the survey. However, four of the returned surveys, or 11.4 percent, were not usable because the respondents did not answer the questionnaire on the grounds that their groups did not fit the term WSRC. The 31 usable survey responses represented 68.8 percent of the total sent. (*See* the Appendix for a list of the WSRCs that responded to the study's questionnaire.)

Twenty of the 31 survey respondents, or 64.5 percent, indicated that a library or information center existed in their WSRCs. Among the survey respondents, 12 have a library, three have an information center, and five have both a library and an information center. (*See* Table I.) The sizes of the library collections vary widely from a few hundred volumes to the 5,500 volumes of the Marguerite Rawalt Resource Center of the Business and Professional Women's Foundation or the 27,893 book and serial titles of the Arthur and Elizabeth Schlesinger Library. However, many of the WSRC libraries and information centers contain valuable resources such as unpublished research manuscripts or information databases. Seven, or 35 percent, of the survey respondents stated that their WSRCs relied solely on their internal libraries and information centers.

Table I

Libraries and Information Centers within WSRCs

Responses (N=31)	Number
WSRCs that have a library	12
WSRCs that have an information center	3
WSRCs that have both a library and an information center	5
WSRCs that do not have a library or an information center	11

Most of the libraries and information centers within the survey respondent group are partly staffed by professionally trained personnel. (*See* Table II.) Seven (35 percent) of this group employ one or more librarians or information specialists. Three WSRCs (15 percent) employ both a librarian and an information specialist. The average staff size of these WSRCs is 8.9 staff members.

Table II

WSRCs with a Library or Information Center that Employ a Librarian or Information Specialist

Responses (N=20)	Number
WSRCs that employ librarian(s)	4
WSRCs that employ information specialist(s)	3
WSRCs that employ both librarian(s) and information specialist(s)	3
WSRCs that employ neither a librarian nor an information specialist	9
No response	1

Definitions were provided for terms such as "library," "librarian," "information center," or "information specialist" to help ensure the validity of the survey results. The definitions were taken from the *ALA Glossary of Library and Information Science* (1983).

It should be noted that a few of the survey respondents objected to being referred to as a "women's studies research center." This was the term used in 1982 by Mariam Chamberlain.[4]

All of the survey respondents fit most, if not all, of the criteria for a WSRC. This is reflected by the user groups, activities, and accomplishments of the organizations. These areas were addressed specifically in the latter portion of the survey, which only those WSRCs with libraries or information centers were asked to complete.

The study indicated that a wide range of user groups utilize the libraries and information centers within WSRCs. By far, the largest group of users mentioned in the study were students (70 percent). (*See* Table III.) Perhaps the main reason for the high use of the WSRC libraries and information centers by students is that half of the centers represented in the survey are affiliated with degree-granting academic programs in women's studies. The number of users in an average one-year period varied widely between the libraries and information centers of the different WSRCs, ranging from less than 100 to several thousand.

Three questions on the survey asked for approximate annual budget statistics for the WSRC as a whole, and for the budget percentage allocated specifically to the library and/or information center. Only half of the relevant group of WSRCs responded to these questions. The annual budget for the Schlesinger Library was given as $541,791. The average annual budget for the nine other WSRCs that responded was $238,888. However, the library or information center is usually allocated only a small percentage of the WSRC's total budget. Many of the WSRCs depend on grant foundation funding that may vary from year to year.

Table III

User Groups of 20 WSRC Libraries and Information Centers

User Groups as Reported by Each WSRC	Number	Percentage
Students	14	70.0
Community members or groups	6	30.0
Faculty	5	25.0
Scholars and researchers	5	25.0
WSRC internal participants and staff	5	25.0
Organizations (social, political, women's)	4	20.0
Business, management, and labor	3	15.0
Development practitioners	2	10.0
Media	2	10.0
None or no response	2	10.0
Policymakers	1	5.0
Secondary school teachers	1	5.0

A checklist of available library and information services and activities was included in a section of the questionnaire, and the WSRC directors or representatives were asked to indicate all relevant areas of involvement. (*See* Table IV.) The survey respondents indicated involvement in almost every service and activity listed. In the computerized services category, the WSRCs specified bibliographic database searching, resource networking, and mailing lists as activities. The two WSRCs that indicated the "other" category used it to indicate general services. Only two WSRCs with either a library or information center did not respond to this section; in both cases, the WSRCs attached a brochure describing their organizations' activities.

The questionnaire's checklist was based on a model for a women's information center developed as the result of a 1973 study, the Women's Information Center, funded by the federal Office of Human Relations Programs and the University of Maryland's College of Library and Information Service.[5] The purpose of the Women's Information Center project was "to assess the feasibility of and develop plans for a special information center to serve students, faculty, and staff women on the College Park Campus." The study also yielded "data about the information needs and information-seeking behavior of women." The project envisioned multiple roles for the women's information center, comparing it to a crisis intervention center, an information analysis center, libraries, and several other information agencies. (*See* Table V.) The WSRC survey results parallel many of the projections made in the 1973 study, a case in point being the importance of data to the WSRC functions.

Table IV
Activities of 20 WSRC Libraries and Information Centers

Activities as Reported by Each WSRC	Number	Percentage
Collection of documents	14	70.0
Collection of data	9	45.0
Processing of documents	7	35.0
Processing of data	7	35.0
Storage of documents	10	50.0
Storage of data	8	40.0
Retrieval of documents	6	30.0
Retrieval of data	6	30.0
Dissemination of documents	8	40.0
Dissemination of data	8	40.0
Publication of documents	9	45.0
Publication of data	6	30.0
Announcements in documents	5	25.0
Announcements in data	4	20.0
Information generation in documents	1	5.0
Information generation in data	2	10.0
Computerized services	8	40.0
Referral by documents	3	15.0
Referral by data	2	10.0
Consultation/advice in women's studies discipline	7	35.0
Consultation/advice in political policymaking	6	30.0
Archives	5	25.0
Other	2	10.0
No response	2	10.0

In the final section of the questionnaire, the WSRC directors or their representatives were asked to write a short statement on the role of their libraries and information centers in relationship to their overall work and goals. Several themes emerged from the directors' statements. First, the WSRC libraries and information centers play a primary role in the collection and dissemination of materials that may be difficult or impossible to find in traditional libraries. This view is expressed in the following survey respondent's statement:

> Our holdings contain many materials not available in the main university library. Much of the literature here is fugitive, so we have had many students, as well as individuals from the community, who were pleasantly surprised with what they came across here. The collection is critical to our own research, as well as that of others.

Table V

Comparison of a Women's Information Center to Other Information Agencies

× = Document
● = Data
? = Possible future service
* = Columns added by author

Activity	Library	Information Center	Analysis Center	Documentation Center	Publication	Clearing-house	Referral Center	Crisis Intervention Ctr.*	W.I.C.*
Collection									
Document	×	×		×		×			
Data		●	●	●		●	●	●	●
Processing									
Document	×	×		×	×	×			
Data		●	●			●			
Storage									
Document	×	×		×	×	×			
Data		●	●			●	●	●	●
Retrieval									
Document	×	×				×	×		
Data		●	●			●		●	
Dissemination									
Document	×	×		×	×	×			
Data		●	●	●		●	●	●	●
Publication									
Document					×				×
Data			●						?
Announcement									
Document		×		×	×				?
Data		●							?
Info. Generation									
Document			×						?
Data			●						?
Service (Spec.)									
Document	×	×		×		×			
Data			●	●					
Referral									
Document	×	×		×		×	×		×
Data						●	●	●	●
Consultation & Advice in Discipline		×	×					×	×
Archives	×			×					●

Andrea M. Burgard, *The Women's Information Center Project. Final Report.* (Bethesda, Md.: ERIC Document Reproduction Service, ED 081 459, 1973), p. 7.

Anne F. Painter. *The Role of the Library in Relation to Other Information Activities: A State-of-the-Art Review.* Washington, D.C.: Army Office of Chief of Engineers, August 1968. TISA Project Report No. 23, p. 23.

Another individual responded:

> Our library is very small and not widely used, but it is essential for our own research, public service, and education programs. And it contains materials, especially clippings and articles, that are not generally available, so it is extremely valuable to researchers working on women and politics.

Second, WSRC libraries and information centers perform a pivotal function in collecting unpublished documents. The following survey respondent's statement illustrates this point:

> Women in development is a new and expanding field where little material is yet published. Thus, a collection of unpublished documents is most valuable to provide background information and data to persons working in and studying about the field.

In some cases, the WSRCs and their libraries and information centers assume the position of advocate. One survey respondent explained that their role is "to help combat the sense of isolation among faculty interested in women's studies" and "to help incorporate works on women into the curriculum."

In summary, the WSRC directors believed the role of the WSRC library to be threefold:

1) To play a primary role in the collection and dissemination of unpublished and published materials that are difficult to find in traditional libraries (for example, fugitive literature and vertical file materials).

2) To perform an important function in collecting unpublished documents (for example, data of research in progress and unpublished documents in new and expanding fields).

3) To help combat a sense of isolation among faculty interested in women's studies, and to help incorporate work on women into the curriculum (for example, through human resource networking and supporting teaching and research in women's studies).

The results of the survey revealed insights into the nature and role of libraries and information centers within major WSRCs. Characteristics such as size, staffing, activities, and purpose were explored. These findings were imparted at the 77th Special Libraries Association Annual Conference in Boston in June 1986.

The encouraging response of the audience at the SLA Conference, and later from the SLA publishing office, led to further investigation into the findings of the survey. Follow-up query letters were sent to all of the WSRCs in the original survey that indicated the presence of a library or information center. A visit was made to the Schlesinger Library. During that visit an interview was held with the library's director, Patricia Miller King, and a tour of the library facilities was conducted. In addition, a review of the literature on WSRCs and women's studies was made covering the period 1970–1986. (*See* Selected Bibliography.)

Most of the literature on WSRCs and their libraries and information centers was found in women's studies journals and small presses. Only a few articles and books were found in the library literature. Two main scholarly sources emphasize the women's collection in large libraries: *Women's History Sources: A Guide to Archives and Manuscripts in the United States*, edited by Andrea Hinding, and *Women's Collections: Libraries, Archives, and Consciousness*, edited by Susan Hildenbrand. Although these two sources are excellent, they do not give much coverage to the smaller centers. Many of the small centers are members of NCRW and WREI, and have played a significant role in the development of women's studies in the last 16 years or more. The preceding study is intended to highlight the role of the NCRW, WREI, and its diverse membership.

The chapters that follow trace the activities of the major WSRCs in regard to their libraries and information centers, advocacy, and publishing. The final chapter reports on the work of the WSRCs engaged in developing a National Women's Studies Database.

References

1. Mariam Chamberlain, "National Council for Research on Women," *Women's Studies Quarterly*, 1 (Spring 1985), pp. 33–35.

   Mariam Chamberlain, "A Period of Remarkable Growth: Women's Studies Research Centers," *Change*, 14 (1982), pp. 24–29.

   Mariam Chamberlain, "Where the Think Tanks Are—20 Research Institutes," *Ms.*, 8 (1979), pp. 72–73.

2. Alice Sizer Warner, "Miss, Mrs., Ms. Radcliffe College's Schlesinger Library," *Library Journal*, 99 (1974), pp. 33–35.

   Barbara Haber, "The New Feminism: Implications for Libraries," *RQ*, 20 (1980), pp. 76–78.

   Renee Gold, "A Room of One's Own: Radcliffe's Schlesinger Library," *Wilson Library Bulletin*, 55 (1981), pp. 750–755.

3. Women's Research and Education Institute (WREI). Congressional Caucus for Women's Issues. *A Directory of Selected Women's Research and Policy Centers*. Washington, D.C.: WREI, 1983.

4. Mariam Chamberlain, "A Period of Remarkable Growth: Women's Studies Research Centers," *Change*, 14 (1982), p. 24.

5. Andrea M. Burgard, *The Women's Information Center Project. Final Report*. (Bethesda, Md.: ERIC Document Reproduction Service, ED 081 459, 1973).

CHAPTER THREE
Libraries and Information Centers
Within Women's Studies Research Centers

The work of a significant number of WSRCs is linked to their libraries and information centers. In 1985, the Women's Research and Education Institute (WREI) of the Congressional Caucus for Women's Issues surveyed 29 women's research and policy centers and found that 41.3 percent of the centers consider their library collections a "primary activity" and 37.9 percent of the centers see collection/maintenance of their databases as a "primary activity."[1] In a follow-up survey to the WREI findings, I found that at least 28.1 percent of the 45 existing WSRCs have libraries and/or information centers, and of this number almost half employ professional librarians and/or information specialists.[2] (Post-survey results showed an even greater number of libraries and information centers within WSRCs.)

There are two main categories of materials collected and disseminated by WSRC libraries and information centers. The first main category is unpublished materials, including manuscripts, working papers, records of women's organizations, oral histories, and other materials that may be considered ephemeral. These unpublished materials are often unique to individual WSRC collections.

The second main category of materials collected by WSRC libraries and information centers is that of published materials that are not easily located or readily accessible within traditional libraries, although they may be found there after extensive bibliographic searches. The goals and philosophies of WSRCs concerning the collection of information and the building of a knowledge base for women's studies is illuminated by a brief examination of the history of some of the major WSRCs.

The first effort to create a special center for the preservation of women's history and the study of women's lives occurred in the first half of the twentieth century. The women involved in the early women's movement were concerned that, unless they preserved documents from the Women's Suffrage Movement and other records of women's contributions to American life and history, women's viewpoints and contributions would be lost. Between 1935 and 1940, Mary Ritter Beard, an American feminist and historian, and a group of her associates attempted to establish a World Center for Women's Archives (WCWA).[3] The mission of the WCWA as envisioned by its organizers was very similar to the goals of women's studies centers today, including teaching, sharing of research on women, and linking of scholarship with activism.[4] Although the WCWA was never firmly established due to insufficient financial resources and lack of public support at the time, Beard's efforts helped to bring valuable donations of materials to other libraries, namely the Women's Rights collection at Radcliffe College and the Sophia Smith Collection at Smith College.[5]

Before the idea of a WCWA emerged, black women intellectuals and social leaders demonstrated a special concern for preserving black women's contributions to American life and society. Mary McLeod Bethune was at the forefront of this struggle to collect and preserve a record of black history in general and black women's history in particular.[6] Bethune, an educator and political leader of great influence during the early twentieth century, founded Bethune-Cookman College in 1904 and the National Council of Negro Women (NCNW) in 1935. The NCNW was an organization of black women's clubs and organizations that grew out of the National Association of Colored Women, a powerful organization during the late nineteenth century. In 1927, Bethune issued an urgent call for the collection and preservation of "anything of historical value pertaining to colored women in general and especially of the National Association of Colored Women."[7]

Although Beard and the WCWA attempted to elicit support from the NCNW for the international women's archives, there is evidence that the WCWA's overtures were less than wholly committed. For example, the WCWA organizers did not invite black women to become official sponsors of their project until 1938, three years after the WCWA was founded.[8] Nevertheless, a NCNW Committee on Archives was organized to work with the WCWA. And, after the WCWA

collapsed in 1940, the NCNW Committee on Archives continued to collect materials from distinguished black women and to arrange exhibits and other enterprises. It was not until 1979, however, that a permanent home was found for the NCNW archives with the founding of the Mary McLeod Bethune Memorial Museum and the National Archives for Black Women's History in Washington, D.C.

The first two libraries to have a focused concentration on the study of women's lives and history were established by women's colleges. The Sophia Smith Collection was founded at Smith College in 1942. The Arthur and Elizabeth Schlesinger Library on the History of Women in America began as the Women's Rights Collection in 1943. Many women's colleges have significant institutional and alumnae archives, but Smith and Radcliffe went a step further in collecting archives of women's history that are of national and international importance.

The Sophia Smith Collection began as a "Collection of Works on Women Writers."[9] The collection expanded and developed around the specialty of the intellectual and social history of women. The Sophia Smith Collection's present objective is "to acquire and to preserve substantive primary sources and selected secondary materials that document the lives of women in the United States and throughout the world."[10] Today, the Sophia Smith Collection has holdings that date from 1790.

Major manuscript collections at the Sophia Smith Collection include, among others, the Ames, Garrison, and Hale Family Papers and the personal papers of Dorothy Reed Mendenhall, Florence R. Sabin, Margaret Sanger, Ellen Gates Starr, Mary van Kleeck, Ruth F. Woodsmall, and Dorothy Wrinch. The Collection's holdings on international and national women's organizations are also substantial and varied.

The Women's Rights Collection at Radcliffe College was renamed in 1967 after two of its most ardent supporters, Arthur and Elizabeth Schlesinger. The Schlesinger Library today is the leading authority for research scholars and students seeking information on the history of women's lives in the United States. It has an international reputation among scholars. The Schlesinger Library's users, which numbered only seven in 1949, grew to 3,200 by 1976.[11]

The Schlesinger Library holdings span from the nineteenth century to the present. It includes more than 400 manuscript collections and a book collection of about 30,000 volumes. The book collection includes etiquette books from 1811 to 1982 and more than 4,000 books on cookery and household management. Well-known names in the manuscript collection include Susan B. Anthony, the Beecher-Stowe and Blackwell families, Julia Child, Betty Friedan, Charlotte Perkins Gillman, Emma Goldman, Amelia Earhart, Elizabeth Holtzman, the Lydia Pinkham Medicine Company, and Esther Peterson. The library also has records for many institutions and organizations that are important to women's history. It is the official repository for the records of the National Organization of Women (NOW).

The goals and objectives of the Schlesinger Library have remained basically as they were in the 1940s. The present director of the Schlesinger Library explains this philosophy:

> The papers of prominent women were to be collected, as were the records of women's
> organizations, family papers and other materials illustrating women's domestic roles,
> and records of women's activities in politics and reform; but documentation of women
> in the arts and literature was to be of lesser interest.[12]

From the beginning, the emphasis of the Schlesinger Collection has been on women's politics and social history; the Sophia Smith Collection's specialty has been the arts and intellectual life of women.

The historical collections at Smith and Radcliffe were destined to be virtually forgotten for decades, although a few dedicated individuals helped to carry them through the difficult times. During the 1960s and 1970s, a renewed interest in the women's historical archives emerged as a result of the "second wave" women's movement and a simultaneous revolution in education that

incorporated ethnic and women's studies into college curriculums. These social changes created greater numbers of potential users of the Sophia Smith Collection and the Schlesinger Library. As a result of these new demands, the libraries increased staff, expanded and renovated their facilities, broadened their range of services, and launched special projects.

Today, the Sophia Smith Collection is housed with the College Archives in a newly renovated and furnished facility, the Alumnae Gymnasium, the gift of alumnae to the college in 1891. Together, the Sophia Smith Collection and the College Archives form one independent department.

More than 800 individuals were registered users of the Sophia Smith Collection in 1982-83.[13] Since the mid-1970s continuous outreach programs have been enacted to attract users to the facility. The department has sponsored occasional major conferences, such as the Margaret Sanger Centennial Symposium in 1979-80. An annual series of Interterm Symposia featuring distinguished lecturers has been offered since 1976. A series of subject bibliographies is offered free upon request from the Sophia Smith Collection, and three comprehensive catalogs of selected sources in the Collection are offered for a small fee.

Radcliffe College increased its attractiveness to scholars and others interested in the study of women's lives and history by joining with the Schlesinger Library on the Radcliffe campus an independent research program for women scholars and a national repository for data concerning the study of American women. The Mary Ingraham Bunting Institute of Radcliffe College was founded in 1960 as the Radcliffe Institute for Independent Study. The Institute awards post-doctoral fellowships primarily to women scholars, scientists, artists, and writers. Recipients are given the supportive environment of the Institute and resources to complete work of significance to their fields and to their own careers. The Henry A. Murray Research Center, a national repository for data collected by social scientists concerning American women, was founded in 1976. The Murray Research Center catalog, *A Guide to the Data Resources*, is available for purchase.

The Schlesinger Library moved from small departmental quarters into the extensively renovated former college library building of Radcliffe College in 1967. The Schlesinger Library initially shared this building with the Bunting Institute and the Murray Research Center, but has twice expanded the space it occupied to meet the requirements of its growing collection and services. In 1986-87, an extensive modernization of the Schlesinger Library was begun, and the Murray Research Center relocated to facilities within the Radcliffe Research and Study Center. The modernization project of Schlesinger included new reading rooms; a centralized catalog, reference, and reader services area; additional open stacks, compact shelving in climate-controlled storage vaults; a conference room and additional office space; facilities for computer-assisted cataloging, reference, and management; facilities for the establishment and research use of a new audiovisual archive; and improved access for the handicapped.

Since 1973, many major projects to improve the collection and user services have been undertaken by the Schlesinger Library with the support of grants from the National Endowment for the Humanities, the National Historical Publications and Records Commission, the William Bingham Foundation of Cleveland, Ohio, and other gifts and grants to Radcliffe College for the Schlesinger Library. Numerous valuable manuscript collections of historical and contemporary importance in the areas of education, careers, family lives, and health have been processed for improved control and access. More than a dozen manuscript collections are now available on microfilm or microfiche through interlibrary loan, including the papers of the Beecher-Stowe and Blackwell families, Charlotte Rankin, and Emma Goldman. Some of the Schlesinger Library's manuscripts are made available through various publishers. The Schlesinger Library has been involved in several large oral history projects, including "The Black Women Oral History Project," "Women in the Federal Government: Documentation of Their Contributions Through Oral History," and "The Cambodian-American Oral History Project."

Between 1978 and 1985 the Andrew W. Mellon Foundation provided grants to dozens of scholars who requested financial support to utilize the Schlesinger Library and Henry A. Murray Research Center. The Schlesinger Library also sponsors colloquia, conferences, programs, and presentations

relating to its holdings; these attract hundreds of participants each year. The complete finding aids for the holdings of the Schlesinger Library as of October 1983 were published by G.K. Hall in 10 volumes in 1984.

In 1956 the Marguerite Rawalt Resource Center of the Business and Professional Women's Foundation (BPWF) was founded. The Rawalt Resource Center was one of the first of its kind to focus on building a collection for and about working women. It was a forerunner of many other centers to address the special needs of the new feminists for special libraries and information centers.

A brochure outlining the goals and programs of the BPWF states that the Foundation recognized early that "Knowledge is Power."[14] The BPWF has developed into an information authority on economic issues concerning working women that is utilized by employers, educators, policymakers, and media throughout the nation. The expressed aim of the BPWF is to assist working women in achieving economic equity with men by stimulating research toward this end, and ". . .its information serves to document women's advancement, spur new policy initiatives, and educate the public about the changing world of working women."[15]

The Rawalt Resource Center collection consists of approximately 5,000 book titles, 100 journals and newsletters, microfilmed dissertations and special sound recordings, and an extensive vertical file of clippings, articles, and pamphlets. In 1985 the vertical file contained approximately 12,000 items. Materials cover a wide range of economic issues based on the status of women in society, labor policy and economics, work and family, and workplace trends and their effects on women workers.

The information and referral services of the Rawalt Resource Center are extensive and dynamic. The Center is open to the public, although circulation is limited to interlibrary loans and staff. In addition to in-person inquiries and visits, the Center answers nearly 1,500 telephone and mail queries annually. The Rawalt Center produces and distributes information packets on current topics for a small handling fee and "Factsheets" free upon request. Patrons are encouraged to keep up-to-date with literature relating to women and work by registering for the mailing list; they will receive the Center's bimonthly, annotated acquisitions list.

The Center for Continuing Education of Women (CEW) at the University of Michigan was begun in 1964 as one of the first university women's centers in the country. The CEW approach to assisting women in career and employment decision making encompasses counseling, advocacy, research, and information dissemination. The CEW is accomplished in its goals and has become a national model among university women's centers.

Since its inception, the CEW has kept statistical data based on its records of formal counseling visits, which presently number approximately 1,800 individual counseling appointments per year.[16] Annual participant data are used for program planning to document changes in the user population and for research development. According to one report,

> . . . the typical woman coming to the Center in the early years was probably a housewife in her early or mid-thirties, whose children were moving out of the preschool stage; she was considering a return to school to complete her education or to earn a degree in preparation for employment when the time was right. Today, a significant number of CEW participants are somewhat younger women—late twenties or early thirties—already employed. Their concern is not with making the initial move from homemaking to paid employment or a return to school, but rather with selecting a more appropriate, satisfying, or promising career path.[17]

Recent research projects utilizing CEW data and funded by the Ford Foundation focused on the transition from education to employment and the factors affecting career development across the life cycle, including the interrelationships of career satisfaction, marital and parental roles, and psychological well-being. Center data have also been used by graduate students for studies of educational and career choices of returning women, achievement orientation in women, and problems of older students. The CEW sponsors an annual Visiting Scholar in Adult Development, as well as other scholarship programs.

The CEW library serves a dual function as a support to education and career counseling and as a thematic research library. In addition to a circulating collection of about 1,000 books, the library houses a large reference collection of pamphlets, vocational and curriculum materials, dissertations, government documents, periodicals, conference papers, journal articles, clipping files, and reports from other centers and professional groups. The subject range of the library covers the history, status, employment, and education of women. The CEW also publishes various research reports, working and statistical papers, and a newsletter.

The Women's Studies Research Centers that emerged during the 1970s had two major concerns: (1) action-oriented research and (2) dissemination of information to targeted audiences and the general public. The Feminist Press, which has both a library and an information center, was founded in 1970. It is the leading source of information about women's studies programs in the United States, and it has contributed directly and indirectly to the growth in publishing of women writers and in feminist publishing over the last two decades.

The Feminist Press Library contains approximately 2,000 books, a vertical file on the women's studies programs offered in the United States, and a major collection of international "fugitive" materials on women's education. The collection reflects the research interests of the Press, which include women's studies and patterns of education for women, "lost" literature by and about women, the status of women's studies programs, the status of centers for research on women, and the literary works and fine arts by and about disabled women.

The Feminist Press, best known for its publishing contributions, has strong programs in independent research and public service. *Everywoman's Guide to Colleges and Universities*, the feminist reference guide to American colleges and universities, was first published in 1982 by the Feminist Press after two years of collecting data about campus environments for women. Another project by the Press centered around a search for literature and visual arts by and about disabled women artists and resulted in its 1986 publication, *With Wings*, a collection of creative writing. The Press is also responsible for the production of curriculum materials for primary and secondary school teachers. *Women's Lives/Women's Work*, a series of 12 books and 12 teaching guides on the new scholarship on women for school teachers, was the product of seven years of extensive research on high school library history and literature curriculum.

In 1986, the Feminist Press staff of 15 and its organization moved to new facilities at the City University of New York after 16 years on the campus of the State University of New York/College of Old Westbury.

The Project on the Status and Education of Women of the Association of American Colleges was founded in 1971. It is the oldest national project established to promote equality for female students, faculty, and administrators in higher education. The Project serves as a unique liaison among academic women, educational institutions, federal policymakers, and women's organizations. One of the Project's promotional brochures states:

> Our basic assumption is that there are many people of good will—administrators, faculty, students, government personnel, and persons in educational and professional organizations—who will make better decisions if they have the best information available.[19]

The Project on the Status and Education of Women maintains a library and an information center. It acts as a clearinghouse for the public and answers more than 15,000 requests for its publications and information each year. Work focuses on topics such as Title IX and other federal legislation effecting women on campus, equal employment, sexual harassment, women in the curriculum, and sex bias in research. The Project publishes a quarterly newsletter, *On Campus With Women*, and since 1971 has published more than 100 topical research papers.[20]

The Project is funded mainly by private grants, but it receives some public support as a result of its affiliation with the Association of American Colleges. Major support has come from the Carnegie Corporation of New York and the Ford Foundation, the Fund for the Improvement of Postsecondary

Education, the International Paper Company Foundation, the National Science Foundation, and the Women's Educational Equity Act Program. Many individuals also contribute through donations.

Another early entry among the centers specializing in women's studies research was the Center for the American Woman and Politics (CAWP), founded in 1971 as a unit of the Eagleton Institute of Politics at Rutgers University. CAWP supports research, education, and information dissemination concerning women's political participation; it works to increase knowledge of women's political participation through a number of incentive programs, including a National Information Bank on Women in Public Office and an information service.

The National Information Bank is based on a census and survey, conducted by the CAWP in 1975 and again in 1977, of elected women serving in municipal, county, state, and federal offices. The 1975 census resulted in the first comprehensive county of women serving at county and municipal levels of government.[21] The National Information Bank strives to keep a current count of women public officials in all 50 states. The National Information Bank maintains biographical information on each government official, as well as attitudinal data about political women. This data is disseminated to a wide range of users, including media, political institutions, government agencies, and scholars.

CAWP offers an information service that includes a subscription to *News & Notes*, a newsletter issued three times a year. Participants also receive announcements, resource ideas, fact sheets, and reports about the number, status, and impact of women in public office. CAWP's research activities are regularly reported in its publications.

CAWP maintains a special library collection on women's political participation. The collection is available for use by students and faculty of Rutgers University and other interested individuals. The CAWP collection is composed of: (1) periodicals; (2) published and unpublished papers, reports and articles; and (3) a collection of books and other monographs including government documents. The book and monograph collection has more than 600 titles and is catalogued by author and title. Six hundred published and unpublished papers are catalogued using a special women's studies thesaurus developed by NCRW and BPWF. (This special thesaurus will be discussed in Chapter 6.) The center also maintains a subject heading listing for its vertical file materials.

By the mid-1970s an increasing number of centers specializing in the study of women's issues or feminism were introduced in the United States. Many of the women's resource and research centers appeared on university and college campuses as an offshoot of and support to women's studies programs. Such was the case with the Center for the Study, Education, and Advance of Women at Berkeley (1972), the Center for Research on Women at Wellesley (1974), the Center for Research on Women (later renamed the Institute for Research on Women and Gender) at Stanford University (1974), and the Women's Studies Research Center at the University of Wisconsin—Madison in 1977. Several of these centers have small resource collections for the internal use of their researchers, and all publish working papers of their scholars and affiliates.

The private sector has also produced a number of feminist research centers. The Center for Women Policy Studies (CWPS) was organized in 1972 as a nonprofit corporation directed towards feminist policy research. Its research work focuses on women and credit, women in the criminal justice system, and the economic status of women. CWPS publishes *Response*, a bimonthly publication on family violence.

The International Center for Research on Women (ICRW) is a nonprofit institution established in 1976 to increase women's economic participation in developing countries. The ICRW investigates the critical aspects of women's economic roles, provides technical assistance to development agencies in the design and evaluation of employment and income-generating projects, translates research findings into policy and program recommendations, and conducts educational programs.

The ICRW operates a resource center with more than 6,000 published and unpublished papers, government documents, monographs, and UN publications. The resource center is open to the public by appointment only.

The Equity Policy Center (EPOC), founded in 1978, is a nonprofit research, communications, and educational group that collects data and conducts policy analysis on issues of economic development and social change that have a differential impact on men and women. The EPOC maintains a library of approximately 2,000 items of primarily unpublished materials; it also publishes its own conference proceedings, working papers, and reports.

The Catalyst Library was established to support the internal research of Catalyst, a national nonprofit advocacy organization. The library was started in 1975 with a three-year grant from the Andrew W. Mellon Foundation. Subsequent grants from the Mellon Foundation enabled Catalyst to expand the service of the library to include an audiovisual center and database service.

The Catalyst database file, called Catalyst Resources for Women and available through BRS (Bibliographic Retrieval Services) consists of bibliographic citations and abstracts of a wide range of materials, both ephemeral and published. The database is particularly strong on issues involving the dual-career family, re-entry women, and women's service on and to corporate boards.

The early 1980s produced greater growth and increased specialization among WSRCs. In 1981, Spelman College in Atlanta received a grant from the Charles Stewart Mott Foundation to establish a Women's Research and Resource Center, the first of its kind on a black college campus. The major objectives of this center are curriculum development in women's studies, community outreach to black women, and research on black women. The center is also responsible for maintaining the Spelman Archives within its own facilities for use by students, faculty, and scholars interested in researching the education of black women. The Spelman College Women's Research and Resource Center publishes a scholarly journal entitled *Sage* and a newsletter.

In 1981, the Girls Clubs of America, Inc., created a National Resource Center in Indianapolis. The Center conducts research on informal educational programming for girls ages six to 18 and acts as a clearinghouse for its 240 clubs across the U.S., as well as for schools, researchers, women's groups, youth-serving agencies, and the press. Its resource collection reflects Girls Club advocacy areas such as adolescent sexuality and development, educational equity, and girls in sports. The Resource Center distributes "Standard Resource Packets" of related information and statistics.

Three specialized WSRCs opened in 1982. The Center for Rural Women was created at Pennsylvania State University. Duke University, in North Carolina, established the Women's Studies Research Center to promote research in North Carolina, South Carolina, and Virginia. The Center for Research on Women at Memphis State University was established to study Southern women and racial–ethnic American women's studies. Memphis State's Center has been a test site for the NCRW in the development of a women's studies thesaurus, which it has used to index more than 1,000 bibliographic citations and more than 200 descriptions of works-in-progress.

It is evident that WSRCs have made available to researchers a large quantity of published and unpublished feminist materials and materials about women that otherwise would have been lost. WSRCs have experienced great success in providing bibliographic information and resources for women's studies curriculum development and feminist research.

Because women's studies is a broad, interdisciplinary field, bibliographic searches even for published materials is often extremely difficult using conventional methods. One women's studies bibliographic professional explains:

> Again, interdisciplinary searches are often best handled with machine-accessible techniques, particularly when the search can employ cross-database of multi-file searching. For example, recent searches on topics in women's studies involved anywhere from eight to 11 files for the most useful coverage. For good information on the topic of abortion as a political issue, one might profitably search the following files: Population Bibliography, United States Political Science Documents, the Magazine Index, both ERIC files, Social Science Citation Index, Sociological Abstracts, Psychological Abstracts, the Public Affairs Information Service, the National Criminal Justice Reference Service, and the MEDLINE file. When reviewing the results,

however, much winnowing of the output was necessary, but key material was found in each file.[22]

Bibliographic searches for women's studies, as indicated in the above observations, are complicated by their interdisciplinary nature, ambiguity of terms, and their sometimes sexist or gender-stereotyped language. WSRCs are sensitized to the interdisciplinary nature of women's studies and the ambiguity that is sometimes a part of it. They have developed specialized areas of expertise within the broader women's studies field. Some of the larger WSRCs have created their own indexes and thesauri. A number of the centers, such as a group within the NCRW consortium, are working towards building a shared women's research database using computer technologies.

WSRC libraries and information centers have published bibliographic information in print and in machine-readable database formats. Their efforts have led to greater distribution and more efficient dissemination of information on women's studies and issues. Many WSRCs are considered by policymakers, the media, and others to be the authority in their specific research areas. In many respects, WSRCs have built their own information network.

References

1. Women's Research and Education Institute (WREI). Congressional Caucus for Women's Issues. *A Directory of Selected Women's Research and Policy Centers.* Washington, D.C.: WREI, 1983.

2. Grace Jackson-Brown, "Libraries and Information Centers Within Women's Studies Research Centers," paper presented at the 77th Annual Special Libraries Association Conference, June 9, 1986.

3. Susan Hildenbrand, "Women's Collections Today," *Women's Collections: Libraries, Archives, and Consciousness,* Susan Hildenbrand, ed., New York: The Haworth Press, 1986, p. 2.

4. *Ibid.*

5. *Ibid.*, p. 3.

6. Bettye Collier-Thomas, "Towards Black Feminism: The Creation of the Bethune Museum-Archives," *Women's Collections: Libraries, Archives, and Consciousness,* Susan Hildenbrand, ed., New York: The Haworth Press, 1986, p. 44.

7. *Ibid.*

8. *Ibid.*, p. 45.

9. Mary-Elizabeth Murdock, "Exploring Women's Lives: Historical and Contemporary Resources in the College Archives and the Sophia Smith Collection at Smith College, " *Women's Collections: Libraries, Archives, and Consciousness,* Susan Hildenbrand, ed., New York: The Haworth Press, 1986, p. 70.

10. *Ibid.*, p. 68.

11. Patricia Miller King, *Fortieth Anniversary Report: The Arthur and Elizabeth Schlesinger Library on the History of Women in America,* Cambridge, MA: Radcliffe College, 1983 (?), p. 7.

12. *Ibid.*, p. 8.

13. Murdock, "Exploring Women's Lives: Historical and Contemporary Resources in the College Archives and the Sophia Smith Collection at Smith College," p. 72.

14. Business and Professional Women's Foundation, "Information on Women in the Workforce from the Marguerite Rawalt Resource Center," one-page flyer included in personal correspondence, October 27, 1986.

15. *Ibid.*

16. (Mariam Chamberlain), "National Council for Research on Women," *Women's Studies Quarterly*, 1 (Spring 1985), p. 39.

The University of Michigan Center for Continuing Education of Women, 1964–1984: A Report, 1 Nelvia Van't Hul, ed., Ann Arbor, MI: The University of Michigan, 1984, p. 11.

17. "From the 60's into the 80's," *Newsletter, Center for Continuing Education of Women*, 16 (1981), p. 2.

18. (Chamberlain), "National Council for Research on Women," p. 36.

19. Association of American Colleges, "Project on the Status and Education of Women," one-page flyer included in personal correspondence, November 5, 1986.

20. (Chamberlain), "National Council for Research on Women," p. 33.

21. Center for the American Woman and Politics, Eagleton Institute of Politics, State University of New Jersey, Rutgers, "CAWP Programs," one-page flyer included in personal correspondence, October 20, 1986.

22. Ellen Gay Detlefsen, "Issues of Access to Information About Women," *Women's Collections: Libraries, Archives, and Consciousness*, Susan Hildenbrand, ed., New York: The Haworth Press, 1986, p. 164.

CHAPTER FOUR
Advocacy and Women's Studies Research Centers

The work of the WSRCs in the U.S. is promoted and assisted by two organizations, the Women's Research and Education Institute (WREI) and the National Council for Research on Women (NCRW). WREI is the nonpartisan research branch of the bipartisan Congressional Caucus for Women's Issues. Established in 1977, WREI forms a bridge between researchers and policymakers concerned with issues of importance to women. It seeks to bring the work of women's research and policy centers to bear on the public policy process by identifying and coordinating research, analyzing the effects of proposed legislation on women, and putting practical and timely analyses in the hands of decision makers.[1]

In 1981, WREI convened a meeting of representatives from 22 research centers and members of the Congresswomen's Caucus, opening the first regular channels of communication between feminist researchers and policymakers.[2] The meeting addressed the current and projected information needs of the two groups. Mechanisms were developed to meet those needs and to promote joint activities.

WREI's current activities include publishing research reports and briefing sheets that are distributed to government representatives, business and labor community leaders, and women's advocacy groups. WREI sponsors conferences and symposia, informal brown-bag lunches and discussion groups, individual research projects, and the development of a computer-based record of research in progress. In conjunction with the George Washington University Women's Studies Program, WREI cosponsors several graduate fellowships on women and public policies.

In 1979, a conference of 20 women's research centers was called by Mariam Chamberlain for the Ford Foundation.[3] An informal network was forged from this initial meeting, and the centers began a regular exchange of information through newsletters, working papers, and other publications.

The National Council for Research on Women, formed in 1981, is an independent association of established centers and organizations that support feminist research, education, and policy. The NCRW forms a working alliance "to bridge traditional distinctions among scholarship, policy, and action programs."[4] Through its member centers the Council links more than 2,000 scholars and practitioners, both men and women. The Council also works to strengthen ties among centers of scholarship abroad and WSRCs in the U.S.

The NCRW's current programs include development of a National Women's Research Database (*see* Chapter 6); sponsorship of seminars, conferences, and roundtable discussions between researchers and practitioners; and development of nonsexist school and college curricula.

The activities of WREI and NCRW follow a philosophy of applied or policy-oriented research, a philosophy based on building a new body of knowledge about women and putting it to work in the decision-making and policymaking processes of society.[5]

The goals of the women's studies movement have always been predominantly political rather than theoretical. Florence Howe, one of the earliest proponents of women's studies, stated that the original goals of women's studies were "consciousness raising" and "compensation" against academic disciplines and popular thought that systematically "trivialized women as a class."[6]

A similar view of women's studies or feminist scholarship is expressed by Ellen Carol DuBois and others, who conducted a study on the impact of feminist scholarship in scholarly journals representing the disciplines of anthropology, history, education, literature, and philosophy:

> At the heart of feminist scholarship in all fields of study is an awareness of the problem of women's oppression and the ways in which academia inquiry has subsidized it, a sense of the possibilities for liberation, and a commitment to make scholarship work on women's behalf.[7]

DuBois *et al.* conducted a quantitative analysis of sample professional and scholarly journals based on publication patterns of articles about women from 1966 to 1980.[8] An average increase of 7.4 percent in the publication of articles about women and feminist issues was found in the five disciplines studied. However, DuBois *et al.* were less encouraged by their critical evaluation of articles from a selected group of the journals from the years 1979 and 1980. In the critical evaluations the researchers looked at factors such as the recognition of a female perspective on relevant issues, the citation of feminist works, and the avoidance of generic masculine pronouns. They concluded that during the publication period studied, "the strength of male bias in all five fields remains undeniable."[9]

A strategy of WSRCs has always been to work for the incorporation of women's lives into the American social consciousness and the educational system. Feminists were encouraged by the enactment of Title IX of the Educational Amendment of 1972, which guarantees equal educational opportunity without regard to sex in all educational programs that receive federal financial assistance. Expectations arose enormously among feminists based on what they hoped could be accomplished for women within the educational system as a result of this legal victory.

In addition to policy-oriented research, formal and informal networking is another means by which WSRCs accomplish their organizations' goals. Networking may involve a simple brown-bag lunch and discussion, or a formal conference around a particular research theme, or a referral by one of the centers of an individual scholar to other individuals conducting similar research. Whatever form networking takes, it has proven particularly helpful to those who teach and research women's studies. Women's studies faculty and feminist researchers often seek assistance from WSRCs as a support advocate for the introduction or integration of women's studies courses into college curricula; WSRCs also serve as a place for sharing mutual interests and concerns.

Many of the WSRCs offer special scholarships and fellowship programs. Awardees are expected to make research contributions or contribute to the work of the centers. Brown University's Pembroke Center for Teaching and Research on Women, for example, offers four annual post-doctoral fellowships with stipends. Pembroke scholars must produce a research project on the cultural constructs of gender, participate in weekly seminars, and present at least one paper.

The Center for the Study of Women in Society, at the University of Oregon, awards a fellowship to one visiting scholar each year. The Business and Professional Women's Foundation offers three scholarship and grant programs for women: the Career Advancement Scholarship Program, The Lena Lake Forrest/BPWF Research Grants, and the Sally Butler Memorial Fund for Latina Research. Other fellowship and internship programs, such as those at Berkeley, Stanford, and the University of Arizona, do not offer stipends but do offer assistance in providing research resources and other benefits.

WSRCs are advocates of outreach programs in information and bibliographic services to help meet the needs of schools, community groups, and businesses. The Southwest Institute for Research on Women (SIROW) at the University of Arizona conducts an exemplary outreach program of information service and dissemination in cooperation with the Arizona Historical Society, the Tucson Public Library, the Arizona Office of Economic Planning and Development, and WREI. SIROW sponsors teacher training programs in nonsexist, multicultural curriculum development that reach educators from schools in Arizona, Colorado, New Mexico, and Utah. SIROW is also a participant in the Western States Project on Women in the Curriculum. The program is funded by the Ford Foundation and is set up to assist four-year colleges and universities in 16 western states in incorporating the new scholarship on women into introductory and core courses in the traditional curriculum.

Another example of a special outreach program is represented by the educational programs offered by the Institute for Women and Work at Cornell University's New York State School of Industrial and Labor Relations. Educational programs for women are offered on both a college credit and noncredit basis at the Institute in association with employers and employee trade unions. For example, courses are offered to promote leadership skills for women interested in trade unionism.

The Stanford V. Lenz Library, a reference library and special collection relating to women and work, is available within the Institute and is open to the public.

In summary, the promotion of women's studies at every level of the American educational system and the interpolation of feminism into social policymaking appears to be at the forefront of research and information activities of WSRCs.

References

1. Women's Research and Education Institute (WREI). Congressional Caucus for Women's Issues. *A Directory of Selected Women's Research and Policy Centers*. Washington, D.C.: WREI, 1983, p. 1.

2. Mariam Chamberlain, "A Period of Remarkable Growth: Women's Studies Research Centers," *Change*, 14 (1982), p. 27.

3. (Mariam Chamberlain), "Where the Think Tanks Are—20 Research Institutes," *Ms.*, 8 (1979), p. 72.

4. National Council for Research on Women, "The National Council for Research on Women," a one-page flyer included in personal correspondence, February 10, 1986.

5. Laura Lein and Peggy McIntosh, "Putting Research to Work: Applied Research on Women," *Working Paper*, 97, Wellesley College, Center for Research on Women, 1982.

6. *The International Encyclopedia of Higher Education*, 1977, ed., s.v. "Women and Higher Education," by Shelia Tobias, pp. 4398–4404.

7. Carol Ellen DuBois, *et al.*, *Feminist Scholarship: Kindling in the Groves*, Urbana: University of Illinois Press, 1985, p. 197.

8. *Ibid.*, pp. 157–194.

9. *Ibid.*, p. 191.

CHAPTER FIVE
Publishing and Women's Studies Research Centers

A major impetus to the growth of women's studies was the publication of a series entitled *Female Studies*, a collection of academic course syllabi and teaching aids. Shelia Tobias, one of the editors of *Female Studies*, said of the *Female Studies* series and its influence on women's studies:

> The syllabi collections, together with some regional conferences among teachers of women's studies, spread the idea and the legitimacy of the enterprise more rapidly than would otherwise have been the case, because already in 1971, student activism was waning, and the universities were about to enter a more cautious and self-protective phase.[1]

The series was first published by KNOW, INC., in 1970. *Female Studies I*, edited by Tobias, features outlines of 16 courses taught or proposed during 1969 and 1970, as well as a ten-course curriculum from San Diego State University, which was the first officially established integrated women's studies program in the United States.[2] *Female Studies II* is an anthology of 61 course outlines and bibliographies collected by the Modern Language Association's Commission on the Status of Women and edited by its chairperson, Florence Howe.[3] *The New Guide to Current Female Studies*, the third volume in the series, was published in 1971. It lists 610 courses at 200 institutions, including 500 instructors—163 in English, 52 in sociology, 84 in history, and the others scattered throughout the remaining disciplines.[4] The series has since ceased publication.

After co-editing the *Female Studies* Series, Tobias taught women's studies courses and helped establish women's studies programs at Cornell and Wesleyan Universities. Tobias is a past president of the Professional Women's Caucus and has been an active member of the Association of American College's Project on the Status and Education of Women.

Howe has also taught women's studies and is a prolific feminist writer. Howe and Paul Lauter co-founded the Feminist Press in 1970 as a nonprofit, tax-exempt educational and publishing organization. They started the Press with less than $100 collected from enthusiastic donors after initial efforts to get commercial publishers interested in publishing books by and about women failed.[5]

The Feminist Press's first book was a children's book entitled *The Dragon and the Doctor* by Barbara Danish (1971). The early emphasis of the Press was to publish sexually neutral, nonstereotyped books for children. The Press gradually expanded its subject specialties to include adult fiction and nonfiction.

Among the rediscovered works by women writers that the Feminist Press has published are Rebecca Harding Davis' *Life in the Iron Mills*, Charlotte Perkins Gilman's *The Yellow Wallpaper*, Agnes Smedley's *Daughter of Earth*, and the Zora Neal Hurston reader, *I Love Myself When I Am Laughing*.

Historically overlooked literary works of many women writers have won new recognition, due in part to the reevaluation of archival materials and the reprinting of works by the Feminist Press and other feminist publishers and in part to distribution to a more socially conscious audience of readers. According to researcher Elizabeth A. Meese,

> The discovery, publication, and analysis of women's archival materials are a necessary beginning to the reassessment of women's place in the literary canon and of the canon itself. Specifically, women's archival materials can aid in clarifying the assumptions that underlie canonization and devising new, more inclusive criteria: in discovering additional writers and works deserving of literary attention and repute; and in developing fuller context in which to understand women's lives and works.[6]

The Feminist Press has a long history of publishing books by and about women of color, including *Brown Girl, Brownstones*, by Paule Marshall; *Las Mujeres*, by Nan Elsasser and Yvonne Tixier Y Vigil; and *We Are Mesquakie, We Are One*, by Hadley Irwin. In 1982, the Press published a black women's studies exposé, *All the Women Are White, All the Blacks Are Men, But Some of Us Are Brave: Black Women's Studies*. The collection, edited by Gloria T. Hull, Patricia Bell Scott, and Barbara Smith, received critical acclaim as a groundbreaking work in black women's studies.

The Feminist Press and several other WSRCs collect and distribute "fugitive" literature. Fugitive literature is defined as "such publications as pamphlets, programmes, and duplicated materials produced in small quantities and of immediate, transitory, or local interest."[7] Literature of this type is often very useful to researchers. In some cases, feminist writings are available only in a fugitive form. For example, the Feminist Press has a major collection of international fugitive materials on women's education. The publication services of the Equity Policy Center and the Women, Public Policy, and Development Project of the Hubert H. Humphrey Institute of Public Affairs collect fugitive materials on women and social development policy.

The Feminist Press and many other WSRCs contribute to publishing through bibliographies. For example, the Rawalt Resource Center and the Project on the Status and Education of Women regularly publish bibliographies. In a field such as women's studies this kind of publishing is essential to communication and research. Deborah S. Rosenfelt, in her essay, "The Politics of Bibliography," explains:

> Whatever the particular bibliographic form, the basic function is obvious: to inform us of materials that we might otherwise not know about. Cumulatively, though, bibliographies and aids to research perform another function: they map the contours of a discipline. In literature, they tell us what to read—by whom or about whom. The listing of a literary or a critical work in those places where scholars look for guidance—annual MLA bibliographies, specialized topical bibliographies, research guides, and publication histories—is analogous to the reporting of a current event in the media: if the event gets coverage, it is news, if it gets none, it is not.[8]

The Feminist Press is publisher of the *Women's Studies Quarterly*, a journal devoted to teaching about women and a media platform for the National Women's Studies Association (NWSA). *Women's Studies Quarterly* provides coverage of issues and events in women's studies and feminist education at all educational levels. It annually reports information on national women's studies programs and centers for research on women, course descriptions and syllabi, notices of grants and scholarships, and books reviews.

The Feminist Press began publishing a new journal, *AFFILIA: Journal of Women and Social Work*, in 1986. *AFFILIA* is the first social work journal with a feminist point of view. This quarterly journal intends to reflect in articles, reports, book reviews, and poetry the impact of the women's movement upon the profession of social work today.

In its 17 years of existence, the Feminist Press has accomplished a great deal in the areas of publishing and women's studies. Many other WSRCs and alternative feminist presses, following the example of the Feminist Press, have joined the field of publishing during the decades of the seventies and eighties.

Many WSRCs publish journals, newsletters, and working papers. Working papers give graduate students and other researchers the opportunity to share theoretical ideas while those ideas are still in a developmental stage. Some centers that publish working papers are the Equity Policy Center, the Wellesley College Center for Research on Women, and the University of Arizona Southwest Institute for Research on Women. Some papers are presented during conferences or colloquiums, and some are printed and distributed nationally to other women's centers, libraries, and individuals.

References

1. Shelia Tobias, "Women's Studies: Its Origins, Its Organization and Its Prospects," *Women's Studies International Quarterly*, 1 (1978), p. 91.

2. Marilyn J. Boxer, "For and About Women: The Theory and Practice of Women's Studies in the United States," *Signs: Journal of Women in Culture and Society*, 7 (1982), p. 664.

3. *Ibid.*

4. Tobias, "Women's Studies: Its Origins, Its Organization and Its Prospects," p. 91.

5. Shirley Frank, "Feminist Presses," *Women in Print II*, Joan E. Hartman and Ellen Messer-Davidow, eds., New York: The Modern Language Association of America, 1982, p. 99.

6. Elizabeth A. Meese, "Archival Materials: The Problem of Literary Reputation," *Women in Print I*, Joan E. Hartman and Ellen Messer-Davidow, eds., New York: The Modern Language Association of America, 1982, pp. 37–38.

7. *The Librarians' Glossary of Terms Used in Librarianship and the Book Crafts*, Leonard Montague Harrod, comp., New York: Seminar Press, 1971.

8. Deborah S. Rosenfelt, "The Politics of Bibliography: Women's Studies and the Literary Canon," *Women in Print I*, Joan E. Hartman and Ellen Messer-Davidow, eds., New York: The Modern Language Association of America, 1982, p. 12.

CHAPTER SIX
A National Women's Research Database

Women's studies scholars and those closely associated with the field realized early on that a new indexing language was needed to organize and index women's studies research that would (1) be free of sexual stereotype and bias and (2) provide expanded and inclusive access to all types of information important to women's studies. By the mid-1980s, feminist linguists and librarians had conducted several studies that criticized many traditional usages of language as male biased and discriminatory against women.[1] Simultaneously, WSRCs and other women's studies alliances began to examine and explore the arising computer technologies as a means to making their collections more useful to their own organizations and more accessible to a wider audience of potential users.

Beginning in 1975, the Business and Professional Women's Foundation (BPWF) convened a group of 22 organizations to discuss how to improve the utilization and accessibility of women's studies resources. Among those initially involved in the discussions were the Federation of Organizations of Professional Women, Radcliffe College's Schlesinger Library, Catalyst, and the Sophia Smith Collection at Smith College. The group formed the Women's Information Services Network and defined the creation of a cooperative bibliographic database as a major objective.

In the late 1970s, the Women's Educational Equity Communications Network (WEECN), with federal funding through the Women's Educational Equity Act Program, produced a series of useful tools to improve access to women's studies resources. Among the tools produced by WEECN was a booklet entitled *Computer Searching: A Resource for Women's Educational Equity*, a leaflet on "Numerical Data Tapes Relevant to Women's Educational Equity," and a three-volume set on *Resources in Women's Educational Equity*.[2]

Perhaps the WEECN's most outstanding product was a tertiary database that merged citations on women's educational equity from 13 separate databases into one file and indexed them with one vocabulary.[3] However, before the WEECN's work was fully completed, its federal funding was cut and the organization dismantled. Nevertheless, some of the WEECN's database work was useful in a future database project by the National Council for Research on Women (NCRW).[4]

Yet another group, the unofficial Women's Studies Database Task Force of the American Library Association, conducted a systematic analysis to document the need for improved computerized retrieval of women's resources beginning in about 1981.[5] They developed standards for evaluating existing databases and the extent to which they accurately indexed and made available resources on women. The Task Force concluded:

> Taken as a whole, the major drawbacks in existing databases are the lack of coverage by both primary and secondary sources of the relevant subjects, the very problematic language barriers, and the inconsistencies in citation formats and search strategies.[6]

In October 1982, the NCRW sponsored a planning meeting to coordinate efforts to improve storage and retrieval of information on women's studies. The meeting was attended by 31 council members and other interested individuals. The discussion highlighted the fact that research on women and information about programs, policies, and curricula had rapidly outstripped their ability to organize, access, and effectively systematize the wealth of resources generated during the 1970s.

At that time, both the BPWF's Rawalt Resource Center and the Catalyst Information Center were pursuing the development of a computerized database system for each of their own collections. Both centers agreed to work in collaboration with the NCRW to help develop a national women's research database. The NCRW and the BPWF organized a Thesaurus Task Force as the first stage of a collaborative national database project. Catalyst was eventually able to offer its center's database nationally through the computerized bibliographic database vendor BRS, Bibliographic Retrieval Services. (*See* Chapter 3.)

The NCRW and BPWF attacked the problem of creating a new indexing language that could be used to organize women's studies research as the first step in developing a national women's research database. The thesaurus project that began in full force in 1983 took four years to complete. The result, in August 1987, was *A Women's Thesaurus: An Index to Language Used to Describe and Locate Information By and About Women*, published by Harper & Row. Financial support for the thesaurus project was provided by BPWF, the Ford Foundation, the Lilly Endowment, and the Prudential Foundation. In kind programming and computer time contributions were provided by Advanced Data Management, developers of the software used to build the thesaurus. Extensive labor time from task force members, subject specialists, and other volunteers was also donated.

The thesaurus project began by combining subject lists, catalog headings, filing system guides, and index terms from 38 research centers, libraries, publishers, and associations. This combined list was shared with librarians, scholars, and policymakers from 11 subject specialties who were asked to add missing terms and definitions, delete terms, suggest preferred terms, and identify potential areas of ambiguity and conflict. The 11 subject areas included: communications; economics and employment; education; history and social change; international women; language, literature, religion, and philosophy; law, government, and public policy; natural science and health; science and technology; social science and culture; and visual and performing arts. The subject specialists' recommendations were then edited to conform whenever possible to the American National Standard Institute's "Guidelines for Thesaurus Construction and Use." According to Mary Ellen Capek, director of the database project,

> We were concerned that the thesaurus accurately describe whatever would be indexed, sought, or filed. We were also committed to making the thesaurus accessible to the broadest possible range of users.[7]

Finally, the thesaurus draft was sent to InterAmerica, a Washington-based contractor, who was responsible for computer data entry and lexicographical editing. Prior to publication, the thesaurus was submitted to three rounds of revisions and testing periods at over 60 research, policy, and advocacy centers in this country and abroad.

A Women's Thesaurus (1987) lists over 5,000 terms organized alphabetically, with cross references to broader terms, narrower terms, and synonyms. Entries also list "do not use" terms and suggest preferred usage (for example, Broken Home, Use SINGLE PARENT FAMILY or Housewives, Use HOMEMAKERS). Page arrangements are designed to lead users into the language, to provide help in locating terms that both refine and expand key concepts.

The NCRW foresees the thesaurus supporting a variety of applications. It is expected to aid indexers and others who create, as well as those who search manual and computerized filing systems. The thesaurus can be used to index all types of materials from books to research articles. The thesaurus is designed for optimum use with computerized bibliographic retrieval systems. Except where pre-coordinated (multi-word) terms are needed for defining a unique concept (such as GENDER GAP or SEX SEGREGATION), the thesaurus is post-coordinated, i.e., terms are separated so that both indexers and users can index or retrieve literature with maximum efficiency in assigning keywords and requesting search terms. Instead of NURSES—SALARIES or HOUSEWIVES AS AUTHORS, for example, a user can index or retrieve literature on these subjects by pairing terms listed separately in the thesaurus: NURSES and WAGES and COMPARABLE WORTH or EQUAL PAY, or AUTHORS and HOMEMAKERS or WAGE-EARNING WIVES or WOMEN WORKING OUTSIDE THE HOME.

The thesaurus may also be used to suggest cross references and narrower terms that can sharpen existing classification and cataloging systems. The thesaurus itself is not intended to replace existing classification and cataloging systems; however, the thesaurus was designed to maintain compatibility with existing systems by utilizing preferred Library of Congress subject headings whenever possible. It is hoped by the NCRW that the thesaurus will enable catalogers working with manual or online card catalogs to add detailed descriptors that will describe their collections more accurately and

provide them with an alternative means of alleviating biases embedded in existing classification systems. The thesaurus can be used as a reference guide for nonsexist use of the language.

The NCRW plans to expand and update the thesaurus periodically for accuracy and currency. The thesaurus already contains some non-English terms where the terms express concepts that do not have precise translations in English. The NCRW is exploring the possibility of translating the thesaurus into other languages or publishing a thesaurus with an "international vocabulary."

The second phase of the NCRW thesaurus/database project involves supporting its member organizations in developing in-house automated library and information systems. One of the Council centers, the Center for Research on Women, at Memphis State University, is utilizing the Council's thesaurus to index the holdings in its collection on black women and Southern women. The database currently contains 2,500+ up-to-date references to books, journal articles, chapters in books, unpublished works (including doctoral dissertations), and nonprint materials.

Computer-based searches of the Center for Research on Women at Memphis State collection are available to scholars, educators, students, policymakers, and the general public through its Research Clearinghouse. This project was initially funded in 1984 by the U.S. Department of Education's Fund for the Improvement of Post-Secondary Education (FIPSE). Memphis State has worked with representatives of the NCRW to develop guidelines for indexing and abstracting using an automated system.

Although funding continues to be a major obstacle, several NCRW member organizations have secured sufficient funds to begin computerizing their collections or compiling information that can be made available online. Among those centers that have made advances in this area is the Business and Professional Women's Foundation, which has begun to abstract, index, and enter their Rawalt Resource Center collection online. Stanford University's Center for Research on Women has begun a project to collect and computerize resources on family law. The HERS Mid-America center is working with the NOW Legal Defense and Education Fund's Project on Equal Education Rights (PEER) to compile database information on successful computer equity programs for women and girls. The Women in Development Research and Information Clearinghouse (WIDRIC) at the University of Minnesota have part of their collection online with the Family Resource Services Database, which is available through BRS.

The NCRW is exploring the compact laser disk with Read Only Memory (CD-ROM) as a possible storage device for a future national women's research database that could combine the databases from its member centers. Another possibility that NCRW is examining is linking the regionally developed database via a computer networking system. Capek explains:

> Our vision is a series of clearinghouses, national and international, that will collect and computerize information in key subject areas. Information will be available in a variety of formats: existing bibliographic citations and abstracts; current data; work in progress; directories of related centers, programs, and resource persons; full texts of relevant documents. These regionally developed and maintained databases can be pooled and made available to broader audiences on disks or clearinghouse computers accessible locally, regionally, nationally, and internationally.[8]

The NCRW formed a Database Steering Committee in 1984 to help coordinate the planning for a national online database and to oversee raising funds for it. The Database Steering Committee includes representatives for BPWF, the Center for Research on Women at Memphis State University, the Schlesinger Library, the Women's Research and Education Institute, HERS Mid-America, and the American Library Association's Committee on the Status of Women in Librarianship, among others.

Undoubtedly, the goal of a national women's research database will be realized in the future. It would facilitate women's studies research nationally and abroad by increasing the field's information power. It may be the key advantage politically and intellectually to help establish women's studies as an academic discipline.

References

1. Robin Lakoff, *Language and Women's Place*, New York: Harper & Row, 1975.

   Joan K. Marshal, *On Equal Terms: A Thesaurus for Nonsexist Indexing and Cataloging*, New York: Neal-Schuman, 1977.

   Sexist Language, Mary Vetterling-Braggin, ed., Totowa, NJ: Littlefield, Adams, 1981.

   Women: In LC's Terms, Ruth Dickerstein, Vicki Mills, and Ellen Waite, eds. Phoenix, AZ: Oryx Press, 1987.

2. Ellen Gay Detlefsen, "Issues of Access to Information About Women," *Women's Collections: Libraries, Archives, and Consciousness*, Susan Hildenbrand, ed., New York: Haworth Press, 1986, pp. 167–168.

3. *Ibid.*

4. Mary Ellen S. Capek, "Wired Words: Developing an Online Thesaurus and Database for Improving Access to Women's Information Resources," *NWSA National Women's Studies Association, Perspectives*, 5 (Winter 1987), p. 1.

5. Sarah M. Pritchard, "Developing Criteria for Database Evaluation: The Example of Women's Studies," *Evaluation of Reference Services*, Bill Katz and Ruth A. Fraley, eds., New York: Haworth Press, 1984, pp. 247–261.

6. *Ibid.*, p. 259.

7. Capek, "Wired Words: Developing an Online Thesaurus and Database for Improving Access to Women's Information Resources," p. 40.

8. *Ibid.*, p. 42.

SELECTED BIBLIOGRAPHY

Boxer, Marilyn J. "For and about Women: The Theory and Practice of Women's Studies in the United States," *Signs: Journal of Women in Culture and Society*, 7 (1982), pp. 661–695.

Burgard, Andrea M. *The Women's Information Center Project. Final Report.* Bethesda, MD: ERIC Document Reproduction Service, Ed 081 459, 1973.

Capek, Mary Ellen S. "Wired Words: Developing an Online Thesaurus and Database for Improving Access to Women's Information Resources," *NWSA, National Women's Studies Association, Perspectives*, 5 (Winter 1987), p. 1, 40–43.

(Chamberlain, Mariam). "National Council for Research on Women," *Women's Studies Quarterly*, 1 (Spring 1985), pp. 33–35.

Chamberlain, Mariam. "A Period of Remarkable Growth: Women's Studies Research Centers," *Change*, 14 (1982), pp. 24–29.

Chamberlain, Mariam. "Where the Think Tanks Are—20 Research Institutes," *Ms.*, 8 (1979), pp. 72–73.

Dickerstein, Ruth, Vicki Mills and Ellen Waite (eds.). *Women: In LC Terms*, Phoenix, AZ: Oryx Press, 1987.

DuBois, Ellen Carole. *Feminist Scholarship: Kindlings in the Groves of Academe*, Urbana, IL: University of Illinois Press, 1985.

Evans, Mary. "Women's Studies Research in the United States: A Review and Discussion," *Women's Studies International Quarterly*, 4 (1981), pp. 221–224.

Galloway, Sue. "Women, The New Feminism: Its Periodicals," *Wilson Library Bulletin*, 47 (1972), pp. 150–152.

Gerstenberger, Donna and Carolyn Allen. "Women's Studies/American Studies, 1970–1975," *American Quarterly*, 29 (1977), pp. 263-279.

Gold, Renee. "A Room of One's Own: Radcliffe's Schlesinger Library," *Wilson Library Bulletin*, 55 (1981), pp. 750–755.

Hildenbrand, Susan (ed.) *Women's Collections: Libraries, Archives and Consciousness*, New York: Haworth Press, 1986.

Hinding, Andrea. *Women's History Sources: A Guide to Archives and Manuscripts in the United States*, New York: Bowker, 1979.

Howe, Florence. "The New Scholarship on Women: The Extent of the Revolution," *Women's Studies Quarterly*, 10 (1982), pp. 27–29.

Hull, Gloria T. (ed.). *All the Women Are White, All the Blacks Are Men, But Some of Us Are Brave*, Old Westbury, NY: The Feminist Press, 1982.

Kirtland, Monika. *Women's Studies: A Bibliographic Essay*, Bethesda, MD: ERIC Document Reproduction Service, ED 180 397, 1978.

Lein, Laura and Peggy McIntosh. "Putting Research to Work: Applied Research on Women," *Working Paper*, 97, Wellesley, MA: Wellesley College, Center for Research on Women, 1982.

McIntosh, Peggy. "Warning: The New Scholarship on Women May Be Hazardous To Your Ego," *Women's Studies Quarterly*, 10 (1982), pp. 29–31.

McRobbie, Angela. "The Politics of Feminist Research: Between Talk, Text and Action," *Feminist Review*, 12 (1982), pp. 46–57.

Marshall, Joan K. *On Equal Terms: A Thesaurus for Nonsexist Indexing and Cataloging*, New York: Neal–Schuman, 1977.

Martin, Wendy and Mary Louise Briscoe. "Women's Studies: Problems In Research," *Women's Studies*, 2 (1974), pp. 249–259.

Mohantz, Chandra Talpade. "On Difference: The Politics of Black Women's Studies," *Women's Studies International Forum*, 6 (1983), pp. 243–247.

Patai, Daphne. "Beyond Defensiveness: Feminist Research Strategies," *Women's Studies International Forum*, 6 (1983), pp. 177–189.

Pritchard, Sarah M. "Developing Criteria for Database Evaluation: The Example of Women's Studies," *Evaluation of Reference Services*, Bill Katz and Ruth A. Farley (eds.), New York: Haworth Press, 1984.

Reuben, Elaine. "In Defiance of the Evidence: Notes on Feminist Scholarship," *Women's Studies International Quarterly*, 1 (1978), pp. 215–218.

Roberts, Helen (ed.). *Doing Feminist Research*, London: Routledge & Kegan Paul, 1981.

Rosenberg, Rosalind. *Beyond Separate Spheres: Intellectual Roots of Modern Feminism*, New Haven and London: Yale University, 1982.

Schmitz, Betty. *Integrating Women's Studies Into the Curriculum: A Guide and Bibliography*, Old Westbury, NY: The Feminist Press, 1985.

Schopp-Schilling, Hanna-Beate. "Women's Studies, Women's Research and Women's Research Centres: Recent Developments in the U.S.A. and in the F.R.G.," *Women's Studies International Quarterly*, 2 (1979), pp. 103–116.

Schuman, Pat and Gay Detlefsen. "Sisterhood Is Serious: An Annotated Bibliography," *Library Journal*, 96 (1971), pp. 2587–2590.

Searing, Susan. *Introduction to Library Research in Women's Studies*, Boulder, CO: Westview Press, 1985.

Simons, Margaret A. "Racism and Feminism: A Schism in the Sisterhood," *Feminist Studies*, 5 (1979), pp. 341–357.

Sizer Warner, Alice. "Miss, Mrs., Ms.: Radcliffe College's Schlesinger Library," *Library Journal*, 99 (1974), pp. 33–35.

Smith, Barbara. "Toward a Black Feminist Criticism," *Women's Studies International Quarterly*, 2 (1978), pp. 183–194.

Stacy, Judith, *et al.* (eds.). *And Jill Came Tumbling After*, New York: Dell, 1974.

Stanley, Liz and Sue Wise. *Breaking Out: Feminist Consciousness and Feminist Research*, London: Routledge & Kegan Paul, 1983.

Tidball, M. Elizabeth. "Of Men and Research: The Dominant Themes In American Higher Education Include Neither Teaching Nor Women," *Journal of Higher Education*, 47 (1976), pp. 373–389.

Tobias, Shelia. "The Study of Women," *Choice*, 8 (1971), pp. 1295–1301.

Tobias, Shelia. "Women's Studies: Its Origins, Its Organizations and Its Prospects," *Women's Studies International Quarterly*, 1 (1978), pp. 85–97.

"Women and Higher Education," *The International Encyclopedia of Higher Education*. San Francisco: Jossey–Bass Publishers, v. 9, 1977, pp. 4380–4420.

Women's Research and Education Institute (WREI). Congressional Caucus for Women's Issues. *A Directory of Selected Women's Research and Policy Centers*. Washington, DC: WREI, 1983.

APPENDIX

National Council for Research on Women and Women's Research and Education Institute Directory of Centers

American Council on Education
Office of Women in Higher Learning
One Dupont Circle
Washington, DC 20036-1193

University of Arizona
Southwest Institute for Research on Women
Modern Languages 269
Tucson, AZ 85721

* Association of American Colleges
Project on the Status and Education of Women
1818 R Street, NW
Washington, DC 20009

Brown University
Pembroke Center for Teaching and Research on Women
Box 1958
Providence, RI 02912

* Business and Professional Women's Foundation
2012 Massachusetts Avenue, NW
Washington, DC 20036

*† University of California, Berkeley
Women's Resource Center
Room 112, Building T-9
Berkeley, CA 94720

University of California, Los Angeles
Higher Education Research Institute
Graduate School of Education
405 Hilgard Avenue
Los Angeles, CA 90024

† Center for Women Policy Studies
2000 P Street, NW, Suite 509
Washington, DC 20036

Center on Women and Public Policy
909 Social Sciences Building
University of Minnesota
Minneapolis, MN 55455

CUNY Graduate School and University Center
Center for the Study of Women and Society
33 West 42nd Street
New York, NY 10036

* Cornell University
Institute for Women and Work
New York State School of Industrial Labor Relations
15 East 26th Street
New York, NY 10010

Duke University/University of North Carolina
Women's Studies Research Center
119 East Duke Building
Durham, NC 27708

* Equity Policy Center
2001 S Street, NW
Washington, DC 20009

*† The Feminist Press
311 E. 94th St.
New York, NY 10128-5603

The George Washington University
Women's Studies Program and Policy Center
Stuart Hall, Room 203
Washington, DC 20052

* Girls Clubs of America, Inc.
National Resource Center
441 W. Michigan Street
Indianapolis, IN 46202

Higher Education Resource Services, Mid-America
Colorado Women's College Campus
University of Denver
Denver, CO 80220

Higher Education Resource
  Services, New England
Wellesley College
Cheever House
828 Washington Street
Wellesley, MA 02181

*† Higher Education Resource
  Services, West
University of Utah
Women's Resource Center
293 Olpin Union
Salt Lake City, UT 84112

The Institute for Research in
  History
432 Park Avenue South
New York, NY 10016

* International Center for Research on
  Women
1717 Massachusetts Avenue NW
Suite 501
Washington, DC 20036

*† Memphis State University
Center for Research on Women
College of Arts and Sciences
Memphis, TN 38152

* The University of Michigan
Center for Continuing Education of
  Women
350 South Thayer Street
Ann Arbor, MI 48109

Center for Advanced Feminist
  Studies
University of Minnesota
496 Ford Hall
224 Church Street SE
Minneapolis, MN 55455

National Association for Women
  Deans, Administrators, and
  Counselors
1325 Eighteenth Street NW
Suite 210
Washington, DC 20036

† National Council for Research on
  Women
47–49 East 65th Street
New York, NY 10021

State University of New York at Albany
Center for Women in Government
Draper Hall, Room 302
1400 Washington Avenue
Albany, NY 12222

University of Oregon
Center for Study of Women in Society
Room 636
Prince Lucien Campbell Hall
College of Arts and Sciences
Eugene, OR 97403

Panel Study of Income Dynamics
Survey Research Center
Institute for Social Research
University of Michigan, Box 1248
Ann Arbor, MI 48106

The Pennsylvania State University
Center for Rural Women
201 Agricultural Administration Bldg.
University Park, PA 16802

Radcliffe College
Mary Ingraham Bunting Institute
10 Garden Street
Cambridge, MA 02138

*† Radcliffe College
The Henry A. Murray Research Center
10 Garden Street
Cambridge, MA 02138

* Radcliffe College
The Arthur and Elizabeth Schlesinger
  Library on the History of Women in
  America
10 Garden Street
Cambridge, MA 02138

* Rutgers University
Eagleton Institute of Politics
Center for the American Woman
  and Politics
New Brunswick, NJ 08901

Rutgers University
Douglass College
Institute for Research on Women
New Brunswick, NJ 08903

Smith College
Project on Women and Social Change
138 Elm Street
Northampton, MA 01063

* University of Southern California
  Program for the Study of Women and
     Men in Society
  Taper Hall, Room 331M
  University Park
  Los Angeles, CA 90090–4352

* Spelman College
  Women's Research and Resource
     Center
  Box 362
  Atlanta, GA 30314

* Stanford University
  Center for Research on Women and
     Gender
  Serra House, Serra Street
  Stanford, CA 94305

  Urban Institute
  Program of Policy Research on
     Women and Families
  2100 M Street NW
  Washington, DC 20037

  University of Washington
  Northwest Center for Research on
     Women
  Cunningham Hall, AJ–50
  Seattle, WA 98195

† Wellesley College
  Center for Research on Women
  Wellesley, MA 02181

  University of Wisconsin, Madison
  Women's Studies Research Center
  209 North Brooks Street
  Madison, WI 53715

  Women's Interart Center
  549 West 52nd Street
  New York, NY 10019

  The Women's Research and
     Education Institute of the
     Congressional Caucus for
     Women's Issues
  1700 Eighteenth Street NW
  Washington, DC 20009

Key — Based on Survey Responses, Spring 1986
* = library
† = information center

Z 675 .W57 J33 1988
Jackson-Brown, Grace.
Libraries and information
 centers within women's

MAR 2 3 1989